J133.14   Cohen, Daniel,
              1936-

           Phantom animals.

$13.95

 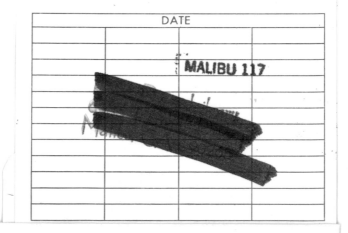

PHANTOM ANIMALS

Daniel Cohen

G. P. PUTNAM'S SONS
New York

G. P. Putnam's Sons, a division of
The Putnam & Grosset Book Group,
200 Madison Avenue, New York, NY 10016.
Published simultaneously in Canada.
Printed in the United States of America.
Book design by Jean Weiss

Library of Congress Cataloging-in-Publication Data
Cohen, Daniel, 1936–
Phantom animals / Daniel Cohen.
p.   cm.
Summary: Presents tales of people who have encountered
ghostly dogs, cats, rabbits, and other animals.
1. Animal ghosts—Juvenile literature.
[1. Animal ghosts. 2. Ghosts.]
I. Title.
BF1484.C64   1991
133.1'4—dc20   90-48105   CIP   AC
ISBN 0-399-22230-8
10 9 8 7 6 5 4 3 2 1
First Impression

To Hugo,
a Clumber spaniel
who is always
in good spirits

CONTENTS

ANIMAL
SPIRITS

The writer Robert Louis Stevenson once said, "You think dogs will not be in heaven? I tell you, they will be there long before any of us."

Perhaps Stevenson was right. On the other hand, it is also possible that some of those canine spirits just hang around here on earth to comfort, or occasionally alarm, their former human companions.

And it isn't just dogs. There are tales of ghostly cats, tigers, horses, cows, even rabbits. And they aren't always friendly. The ghost of a creature as inoffensive as a pet white rabbit was quite enough to scare a couple of brutal murderers to death.

There are fewer stories of animal ghosts than of human ghosts. I'm not sure why this is true. Perhaps it is because there really are fewer animal ghosts. Perhaps it is because animals don't tell ghost stories—at least they don't tell them to us. Who knows what they tell one another? And perhaps it is just because we just don't look at animals the way we look at humans. If we saw a strange human figure suddenly flit across the road and disappear into the darkness, we might at least wonder if what we have seen was a ghost. But if the fleeting figure is that of a cat, even a cat of unusual size and shape, we tend to think, "Well that's just a cat." But is it? Is that barking you hear in the distance coming from a real dog, or something else?

Even so, as you will see, there are plenty of people who think that they have encountered an animal ghost.

Not all of the creatures in this book are ghosts— that is the spirits of once living animals. Some seem to be phantoms that have no connection whatever with any animal that ever lived but just appear in animal form. But like more conventional ghosts, animal or human, they can give you a chill, an uncomfortable feeling that things are not always as they seem, or as they should be.

As is usual with accounts of this type, some are strictly legendary—that is they are stories, and no one really ever believed them. Some are folklore, and people may have believed at one time that they are true. Perhaps some people still believe them to be true, but there is no real evidence the stories actually happen the way they are told. And finally there are those accounts that might—just might—have more than a grain of truth in them.

All types are presented here, strictly for your creepy entertainment. It is not the purpose of this book to make you believe or disbelieve anything. But if you happen to believe the story while you are reading it, so much the better.

THE
DEMON
CAT

The U.S. Capitol building, with its enormous dome, is the most famous and easily recognizable building in the United States. It is practically a symbol of the U.S. government. Visitors to Washington, D.C. usually see the chambers in which the Senate and House of Representatives meet. They stand under the dome in the giant Rotunda and view the life-sized marble figures in Statuary Hall. But there is much about the Capitol that the casual visitor never sees and would not even suspect exists.

Construction on the building first began in 1793. Part of it was completed some seven years later and Congress moved in. Since then the Capitol has been expanded and renovated many times, usually in response to some immediate need, rather than as part of an overall plan. There have been so many serious problems with the building that there has been a rumor that the Capitol itself is cursed! The result is that, aside from the main public areas, the building is a confusing tangle of dark narrow marble halls, winding passageways and countless small hard-to-find rooms. Most confusing of all are the layers of basements and sub-basements all connected by a vast network of underground tunnels. There is even a shuttle subway which connects the Capitol with the nearby Senate and House Office buildings. People with years of experience in the Capitol can still become lost in these underground corridors.

Deep in the Capitol basement is the area in which the catafalque is stored. The catafalque is a raised platform on which the caskets of dead presidents, or others who are given a state funeral in Washington, are placed for the period in which the body is on display in the Capitol Rotunda. The catafalque storage area is said to be home for one of Washington's most alarming specters—the Demon Cat.

About a century ago, the Capitol was overrun with mice and rats. Cats were kept just to hold down the rodent population. As the numbers of rodents decreased, so too did the number of cats. Today there is only one very unusual cat left. It's called the Demon Cat, or sometimes just DC.

Encounters with DC have been reported for many years by those whose job it is to patrol the Capitol corridors at night. This phantom appears only at night, and only when the victim is alone. Sometimes the encounter is fairly benign. Just seeing a large black cat walking along a dimly lit subterranean corridor, where no real cat could possibly be, can be unsettling. Then there are times when a meeting with the Demon Cat can be a far worse experience.

One guard, who didn't want his name to be used, told of meeting DC in the early 1970s. It was a chilly January night. As the guard walked through the corridor, he saw the figure of a large black cat walking toward him. The apparition seemed to actually grow in size as it got closer. As the guard stared into the creature's glowing red eyes, he became paralyzed with fear. Unable to move he watched it swell to the size of a huge tiger. The meowing changed to a roar. Then the animal crouched and sprang with claws extended.

The terrified guard closed his eyes, said a prayer, and thought that he had only a few more painful moments to live. But nothing happened. When he was able to open his eyes again, the guard found that the beast had vanished without a trace.

He only told his closest and most trusted friends of his strange and terrible experience. He was afraid that people might think he had gone crazy or was drinking on the job. He thought that if the story got around he might even be fired.

Some who have encountered the Demon Cat have fainted or run screaming down the corridor. When they tried to bring back others to witness what they had seen, the creature had invariably disappeared. One old guard is said to have had a fatal heart attack brought on by the appearance of DC.

No one has kept an exact record of when the Demon Cat appears. No one could, since many of the
appearances go unreported. But still DC has picked
up a reputation of being something of an omen or
portent. It seems that the Demon Cat appears most
frequently just before some great national tragedy or
when an administration is about to change. Whenever the Demon Cat is seen, those who know the
legend, and believe it to be true, assume that something awful, or at least unsettling, is about to happen.

THE ISLE
OF MAN
MYSTERY

What was Gef—a ghost, an evil spirit, a hallucina-
tion, a hoax? He was called all of that and more. Or
was he what he once called himself, "a little clever,
extra-clever mongoose"? Clever indeed, for this was a
talking mongoose. Whatever he was, the story of Gef
is one of the oddest ever told.

The setting is the Isle of Man, a small island in the
Irish Sea between Ireland and England. It is most famous for being the home of the tailless Manx cat.
The events took place between the years 1931 and
1935, a time when the Isle of Man was more isolated
and remote than it is today.

The center for the story is a farmhouse known in
the Manx language as Doarlish Cashen, or Cashen's
Gap, on the west coast of the island. The construction of the house was unusual and important in the
case. The exterior walls were made from slabs of
slate, faced with cement. The interior walls were a

dark wood paneling. There was a substantial space between interior and exterior walls, which would provide an excellent hiding place for a small animal. It could move all over the house behind the paneling. There were also plenty of knot holes and cracks, through which a hidden animal could spy on those inside the house without revealing its presence. Doarlish Cashen was perched on the side of a small mountain, out of sight of any other farmhouse. It was surrounded by high grass and hedges. Again a perfect hiding place for a small animal that wished to remain unseen.

Then there are the principal actors in this drama: James T. Irving, his wife and youngest daughter. Irving was no simple farmer. He had for many years been a traveling piano salesman, and was both better educated and more traveled than the average Manx farmer. The farm had once been prosperous, but there had been a farming slump, and like many of his fellows Irving had fallen on hard times. He and his family were forced to live frugally but were not destitute. They seemed to have a good reputation for honesty throughout the island.

Mrs. Irving was a rather tall and dignified woman, who clearly ran the house as her husband ran the farm. The daughter Voirrey (Manx for Mary) was a young teenager during the period in which Gef made his appearance. At first Gef seemed to be particularly attached to Voirrey.

The mystery began in September 1931 with some

tapping sounds coming from the attic. That is a fairly standard beginning to a conventional poltergeist account. The next night there was more tapping, the sound of something running and, according to Mr. Irving, "We heard animal sounds: barking, growling, hissing, spitting and blowing."

It sounded as if a small animal had gotten into the house. But very soon it became clear that this was no ordinary animal. Here is what Mr. Irving said:

". . . the animal was making gurgling sounds like a baby when it begins to talk. . . . This was followed by a bark with a pleading note in it. I was amazed. I repeated the noises of various animals: bow-wow—dog, meow—cat. Back came the same sound and the human word for it in a shrill and high-pitched voice, issuing from a very small throat. . . . I was carried away with wonder. An animal was taking lessons from me in human speech!"

Within a few weeks the unseen animal had learned to speak quite well and seemed eager to learn more. It kept pestering Irving, "One more question, Jim, then I will let you go to sleep."

At first Gef, for that is what the invisible animal called itself, frightened Irving. He tried to poison or shoot the creature, but he never got close. Gef insisted that he wasn't evil, but he could be, if treated badly.

One night the Irvings heard groans and choking coming from behind the paneling. Irving thought the creature had finally eaten some of the rat poison he had put down. But after a while the noises stopped and Gef admitted that he had just been kidding. Much to his surprise, Irving was relieved.

After a few months the hostility between the Irvings and their invisible talkative visitor died down and was replaced by a genuine affection.

"I follow Voirrey; Mam (Mrs. Irving) gives me food; and Jim answers my questions," Gef said.

Gef repeatedly expressed the fear that the Irvings would move away. He once promised that he would help make the Irvings rich, but then he said he would not, because if they got rich they would leave him. The creature occasionally left a dead rabbit for the Irvings, who were very fond of rabbit stew. But that is all the material wealth they ever got from him.

While Gef was talkative about many things, he was both reticent and contradictory about what he was and where he came from. For a while he insisted that he was a "ghost in the form of a weasel." Later he said he was "a little clever, extra-clever mongoose." The home of the mongoose is India. Gef once said he had been born in India on June 7, 1852, and had been chased and shot at by natives. That would have made Gef nearly 80 years old, way beyond the known lifespan of a mongoose. He said that he had always been able to listen to people and understand them, but had only recently learned to talk with Irving's aid.

Irving himself said that he had heard that some years before he had purchased the farm, a nearby farmer had released mongooses on the land to keep down the rabbit population. The mongoose is a hardy and adaptable animal, but it's difficult to imagine how these creatures could survive the rigors of a Manx winter. Irving also told the story of how certain Indian holy men had been able to teach mongooses to talk. There is no independent confirmation of this information.

Gef was rarely seen even by the Irvings, and never by anyone else. Voirrey reported seeing him most often. She said he had yellowish fur and a long bushy tail. She described the face as looking like that of a hedgehog, but with a flattened snout. He was said to have very agile "hands" with which he could pick up and throw things. The description generally fits that of a mongoose.

There were a couple of photographs taken of what was supposed to be Gef. "I will have my photograph taken," he announced once. Unfortunately he wasn't a very good subject. The best of the photographs shows what might possibly be a small furry animal, or might be a rock or some other natural object.

If no one aside from the Irvings claimed to have actually seen Gef, quite a number of other neighbors and friends of the Irvings heard him, or something they thought was him. Tales of the remarkable mongoose spread beyond the Isle of Man, and a number of investigators interested in strange and unexplainable phenomena came to visit the remote farmhouse. It was the investigators who made the story of Gef famous throughout the British Isles. None of them reported actually seeing Gef. Only one was even able to talk to the mongoose, though others claimed that they heard sounds that might or might not have been the animal.

They were told that Gef did not limit his activities to the Irvings' house. He visited houses as much as twenty miles away and often brought back stories about what others were doing and saying to tell the Irvings. This made some people uneasy. "That mongoose knows far too much," one complained. Gef's judgment on the activities of the human race was usually pretty harsh.

Gef claimed that he would hitch rides on the local buses by hanging on underneath them. Then he would listen to people talk. The electrician at the bus depot put an electric plate under one of the buses. His aim was to electrocute the nosy mongoose. When Irving warned him, Gef replied, "Oh, I know all about it. It is under Bus 81." Irving checked and found that Gef had been quite correct.

After a few years it became obvious that the Irvings were getting tired of Gef. Voirrey, who had been very fond of him when she was young, finally admitted she "would gladly be rid of him."

Finally the mystery just stopped, without any solution or real ending. In 1935 the Irvings sold Doarlish Cashen and vanished. None of their neighbors, nor the researchers they had spent so much time with, ever heard from them again. The new owner of the farm said that he was never troubled by any strange noises. However, in 1947 he claimed to have shot a queer-looking animal like a mongoose. He was pretty sure it was Gef.

There is one odd postscript: If Gef was a ghost, it seems that he was also afraid of ghosts. Among the many stories Irving told investigators was this one.

He was sitting in bed when he heard Gef talking to his wife and daughter downstairs. After being the object of so many of Gef's jokes, he decided to turn the tables on him. He put a sheet over his head, took off his boots and slipped quietly downstairs. "As I entered the kitchen Gef screamed with fright. . . . When I took the sheet off, he sobbed like a child."

THE BIRD OF LINCOLN'S INN

What is it like to go ghost hunting?

It's not at all like the movies. You can't count on the ghosts to appear on schedule. Screaming phantoms don't regularly patrol the dusty corridors of ancient castles. Sheeted figures don't rise at midnight in misty graveyards.

In truth most real ghost hunting is pretty dull. People sit around waiting for something unusual to happen. More often than not, nothing at all happens. But when it does, then even a simple event can seem very terrifying indeed.

Here is an account of a real evening of ghost hunting that took place nearly a century ago. In keeping with the theme of this book, the ghost in this case turned out to be an animal—or to be more exact, a bird.

In London there is a large group of old buildings located near the law courts called Lincoln's Inn. The buildings are mostly used as chambers or offices for lawyers. Around 1901, when these events took place, a few of the rooms in Lincoln's Inn were rented out as private apartments.

One of these apartments had rather a bad reputation. People who rented it didn't stay long. There were eight tenants in three years. The real estate agent whose job it was to rent the apartment kept lowering the rent. Finally it was taken by a writer who was attracted by the very low rent, and who was not in the least superstitious. He lasted about eighteen months, becoming more nervous and unhappy all the time. Finally he could not stand it any longer, and he moved out. He confided to a friend, Ralph D. Blumenfeld, editor of the newspaper the *Daily Mail,* that "things happened." He never said exactly what "things."

The story interested Blumenfeld, and he asked one of his friends, Max Pemberton, a magazine editor, to help him conduct an investigation. They determined to spend one full night in the apartment to see if "things" really did happen.

The two men went to the third-floor apartment just before midnight on Saturday, May 11, 1901. All the other rooms in the building were lawyers' offices, and on Saturday the place was completely deserted. The rooms in the apartment were empty except for two chairs and a table in the largest of the rooms. The main room had two doors, each leading to a small side room. All the rooms were well lighted.

Said Blumenfeld, "We searched the place thoroughly, closed and locked the windows. . . . There was absolutely no possibility of anyone being hidden anywhere in the rooms. There were no cupboards, no recesses, no dark corners and no sliding panels. Even a black beetle could not have escaped unnoticed."

The two investigators spread powdered chalk on the floors of the two smaller rooms. "This was to trace anybody or anything that might come or go."

Then they sat down at the table in the big room to wait. The doors to both the little rooms were closed. "We were both very wide awake, entirely calm, self-possessed . . . and in no way excited or nervous. It was then about a quarter past midnight."

At seventeen minutes to one, the door to one of the small rooms opened by itself. They heard the door handle click, saw it turn slowly and open. Four minutes later exactly the same thing happened with the other door.

"This is unusual," said Blumenfeld, trying to sound calm.

"We both rose, crossed the room and expecting something, found nothing. The doors closed in the usual way, without opposition or resistance."

Before they closed the doors they noticed that there were no marks in the sprinkled chalk.

Now the watchers were much more tense and alert.

Blumenfeld's report continues: "At 1:32—my watch was on the table with a pencil and slip of paper on which I noted the times—the right-hand door opened again, exactly as before. The latch clicked, the brass handle turned, and slowly the door swung back to its full width. . . . At 1:37 the left-hand door opened as before, and both doors stood wide. We did not rise, but looked on and waited.

"At 1:40 both doors closed simultaneously of their own accord, swinging slowly and gently to within about eight inches of the lock, when they slammed with a slight jar; and both latches clicked loudly."

This happened two more times within the next ten minutes. But the last time the doors opened, the men noticed marks in the chalk on the floor of the two little rooms. They sprang up and went to the doorways to examine the marks.

"The marks were clearly defined bird's footprints in the middle of the floor, three in the left-hand room and five in the right-hand room. The marks were identical, and exactly 2¾ inches in size."

Blumenfeld estimated that they were footprints of a bird about the size of a turkey. "There were three toes and a short spur behind . . . each one was clearly defined, with no blurring of outline or drag of any sort."

The men made sketches of the footprints, and then sat down and waited until half past three, but nothing else happened. At that point they decided to end their vigil and go home.

Blumenfeld ended his account by saying, "I have stated here exactly what happened, in a bald matter-of-fact narrative. I explain nothing, I understand nothing. I am not convinced nor converted nor contentious. I have simply recorded the facts. And the curious thing about it is that my curiosity has not been cured."

A lot of people who have searched for ghosts have felt that way.

For nearly a century now psychical researchers have puzzled over this strange account for the invisible bird at Lincoln's Inn. Some tend to dismiss it as a hoax, or a newspaperman's practical joke. Others have called it "one of the major mysteries of the ghost-hunters' world."

There is one odd little footnote to the story. On May 11, 1901, the night the two newspapermen carried out their experiment, a spirit medium named Mrs. Verrell, who lived some fifty miles from London, received a strange message. She was doing automatic writing; that is she would sit with a pencil on a sheet of paper, and allow her hand to be moved by any "spirit" that took control of her hand. This is a common technique still used by mediums and psychics today.

That night Mrs. Verrell scrawled a drawing of a strange-looking turkey-like bird. Underneath the drawing in Latin was a phrase which roughly translated means "Chalk sticking to the feet has got over the difficulty."

That certainly does nothing to clear up the mystery!

CHAPTER

4

THE
PHANTOM
HOUND

"'Footprints.'"

"'A man's or a woman's?'"

"Dr. Mortimer looked strangely at us for an in-
stant, and his voice sank almost to a whisper as he
answered:

"'Mr. Holmes, they were the footprints of a gigan-
tic hound!'"

Thus we are introduced to the most famous of all
the phantom hounds, in the Sherlock Holmes story
The Hound of the Baskervilles.

The hound is supposed to haunt the Baskerville
family. Holmes reads an old manuscript describing
the first appearance of the demon dog. The evil Hugo
Baskerville and some of his friends have pursued a
poor serving girl out on the moors. Hugo is in the
lead.

"The moon was shining bright upon the clearing,
and there in the centre lay the unhappy maid where

she had fallen, dead of fear and fatigue. But it was not the sight of her body, nor was it that of the body of Hugo Baskerville lying near her, which raised the hair upon the heads of those three dare-devil roysterers, but it was that, standing over Hugo, and plucking at his throat, there stood a foul thing, a great black beast, shaped like a hound, yet larger than any hound that every mortal eye had rested upon. And even as they looked the thing tore the throat out of Hugo Baskerville, on which, as it turned its blazing eyes and dripping jaws upon them, the three shrieked with fear and rode for dear life, still screaming across the moor. One, it is said, died that very night of what he had seen, and the other twain were but broken men for the rest of their days."

Sherlock Holmes provides a perfectly natural explanation for the mystery surrounding the appearance of the hound to a later generation of Baskervilles. And the entire story is, of course, fiction. But Arthur Conan Doyle, the creator of Sherlock Holmes and the hound of the Baskervilles, did not just make up the demon dog. The author had heard tales and legends about such creatures, for tales and legends of phantom dogs abound in the British Isles. Conan Doyle's inspiration was probably The Black Dog of Dartmoor, a sort of demon in the shape of a dog that was supposed to roam the grim moors of Dartmoor.

There were, and are, many other tales of phantom dogs. Not all are as terrible as the Black Dog of Dartmoor, and not all of the sightings of these phantoms go back hundreds of years either. Here's one that comes from 1978:

"One approaches Exford [near Dartmoor] down a long, straight hill and we got there when it was already nearly dark. I was driving and I had the headlights on.

"Then we saw, coming up the hill towards us on the right-hand side of the road, the most extraordinary dog. It was a German shepherd type but with long dirty white hair which stood up around it in spikes, as if frozen. It looked almost transparent. Its eyes were red and glowing. Not many dogs make you exclaim as you pass them and still, when I think of it I get goose bumps.

"We were busy and forgot about it but my husband died in horrible circumstances later that year and my life changed drastically and unpleasantly.

"Later I met someone else who said they had seen this dog and that it also presaged death."

The phantom dog as an omen of death is an old and well established tradition in the British Isles. Usually the dogs are black, very large and shaggy and have glowing red eyes. They roam country roads looking for solitary travelers. The dogs don't actually assault the travelers, often they just glower malevolently at them. But that's enough. The sight of such a phantom is a sign that death is near.

These black dogs are known by a variety of names. In the part of England known as East Anglia the phantom is called Black Shuk. In the north of England it is called Skriker. In the county of Lancashire it is the Trash-hound and in Yorkshire Padfoot. Whatever the name it's an animal no one wants to meet.

However, the phantom is not always an omen of death. Here is a story told by a Mrs. Jewell of her firsthand meeting with a creature called the Black Dog of Torrington. The meeting took place in the 1870s, when the narrator was about ten years old.

Late in the evening she was walking down the road with her father. "It was a moonlit night," she said, "and suddenly a sound of something panting came from behind us, and a great black dog, big as a calf, with great shining eyes came alongside us. I caught my father's hand and cried out. Father said, 'Tis the Black Dog! Hold my hand, don't speak, walk along quietly, and don't cry out.'"

The dog trotted alongside them for about a quarter of a mile. Then father and daughter turned to go into their cottage. The dog showed no further interest in them and continued on down the road. The girl's father said that he had seen the mysterious black dog many times but had never known it to harm anyone.

Mrs. Jewell added that later in life she also saw the dog several times, but never again at close range. She insisted that many other people in her district had also seen the dog, but would not talk about it with outsiders because they feared being ridiculed.

Some of these phantom dogs were considered downright helpful. In the early years of this century a man named Jonnie Greenwood told of having to ride through a dark wood one night. As he entered the wood he was joined by a large black dog. He had never seen it before, and did not know where it came from. The dog simply walked alongside him until he came to the edge of the wood. Then it disappeared; he had no idea where it went. On the way back, the dog joined him once again as he entered the wood, and left when he emerged.

Some time later a couple of condemned criminals said that they had intended to rob and murder Jonnie that night in the wood. When they saw a large dog with him they decided that man and dog together might be too much to handle.

Another tale was told by some fishermen who were waiting for the skipper of their boat to go out for a night's fishing. They waited all night, but the skipper never showed up. Early in the morning there was a sudden storm in which the boat might well have been lost if it had put to sea as originally planned. When the skipper finally got to the dock he said that his way had been blocked by a large black dog, which would not let him pass. The dog probably saved the men's lives.

A more typical black dog story comes from a place called Tring in Hertfordshire, England, at a spot where legend had it a woman was once hanged for witchcraft and a demon dog appeared from time to time. This account comes from the early nineteenth century.

A man and his companion were riding home in a cart late one night when they passed the accursed spot. There was a sudden flash of light.

"What was that?" the man cried out.

"Hush," said his companion, and he pulled the horses to a stop.

"I then saw an immense black dog just in front of our horse. It was the strangest-looking creature I ever saw. He was as big as a Newfoundland dog, but very thin and shaggy. He had long ears, a long tail, and eyes like balls of fire. When he opened his mouth we could see long teeth. He seemed to grin at us. In a few minutes the dog disappeared, seeming to vanish like a shadow, or to sink into the earth."

Peel Castle on the Isle of Man was the home of the famous phantom dog known as Moddey Dhoo. It was a great shaggy black dog, which used to come into the guard room in the castle. No one knew who it belonged to, or how it got into the castle. But it was such a fearsome-looking creature that no one had the courage to challenge it.

Then one night, a guard who had been drinking walked into the guard room to mock the dog. He shouted that the dog should follow him into the corridor. Silently the dog did just that. There was a terrible scream, and the guard staggered back into the room, ashen faced and trembling. He lived only three days, and he was never able to speak a word about what had happened. Moddy Dhoo was never again seen at Peel Castle.

Several old English families, like the fictional Baskervilles, are supposed to be cursed with a phantom dog that appears when someone in the family is about to die. A small white dog was reputed to appear before every execution at the notorious Newgate prison in London. It was seen in the prison yard. No one could explain how it got in or out.

Throughout the British Isles there is a tradition that graveyards were guarded by a spirit in the form of a black dog. The creature was often called the Church Grim. Though the black dog was supposed to protect from the Devil those recently buried in the graveyard, it was considered to be extremely bad luck for any living person to see the dog. In fact, it was believed that anyone who saw one of these graveyard black dogs was fated to die within a year.

PHANTOM LIONS

In December of 1877 young Mary Crane and her boyfriend were walking to her home near the village of Sun, Indiana. The couple's path took them through a patch of woods. Upon entering the woods Mary experienced a momentary stab of fear. There had been rumors of a lion, or some sort of large cat being sighted in the vicinity.

Mary shook off her fear as being foolish. She knew very well that there were no wild lions in Indiana. She also knew how people could exaggerate the simplest things. Still Mary did clutch her young man's hand a little more tightly.

As they walked they heard a terrible shriek behind them. Turning, they saw a pair of glowing eyes approaching rapidly. Behind the eyes was something "big as a good-sized calf, with a tail as long as a door." That was enough. The couple broke into a run, the young man proving to be the faster runner.

The big cat caught up with Mary Crane and tore at her dress with its claws.

She fainted and when she awoke she found the thing standing over her licking her face. Mary just shut her eyes and prayed. After an agony of waiting she heard voices coming from the direction of the village. The young man had aroused some of the townsfolk, who came to rescue Mary if they could. The sound of human voices seemed to frighten the animal, for it ran off without hurting her. Mary Crane was left with nothing worse than a torn dress and some very scary memories. No trace of a big cat was ever found near Sun, Indiana.

In 1917 people in central Illinois reported seeing something that looked like "an African lion." According to one report, the lion jumped out of the grass onto a car, then slid off and ran away. The central Illinois beast was named—for no particular reason—"Nellie the Lion." Despite repeated searches, no material evidence of Nellie was discovered, nor was there a clue to where she might have come from or where she went to.

A mysterious giant black cat was reported near Cairo, Illinois, in April, 1970. The press called it a panther, but as with Nellie the Lion, no real big cat could be found.

In the fall of 1981 the people of Cape Cod, Massachusetts, reported the appearance of some sort of large and catlike creature. The most complete description was given by William and Marsha Mendeiros of the town of Truro, who said they saw it on the beach, about fifty feet from where they stood.

"It had a very definite long ropelike tail like the letter J. It hit the ground and went up. We figured it was about as tall as up to our knees and weighed 60 to 80 pounds.

"We were frightened and froze. He was in the path and didn't see us at first. As we made some noise he turned and we saw his face with short ears."

The creature made no attempt to attack or run, but just sauntered easily into the nearby woods and was lost among the trees.

There is a large cat native to the United States. It's the American mountain lion, sometimes called the cougar, panther, puma or half a dozen other names. Though the animal is quite rare today, it once ranged fairly widely throughout North America, and not only in the mountains. But it is highly unlikely that a real mountain lion attacked Mary Crane in Indiana, and even less likely that one was roaming around Cape Cod in 1981.

Other possible explanations are that the animal escaped from a zoo or a circus or was someone's pet on the loose. Mountain lions are occasionally kept as pets, though the practice is most definitely not recommended. Also ocelots, much smaller wild cats from South America, enjoyed brief popularity as pets in the United States—until people found out that they are very hard to handle. The "escaped wild animal" theory is the first one checked out whenever a rash of mysterious big cat sightings are reported. None of the sightings have ever been connected to any escaped animal.

What makes the phantom lion stories particularly intriguing is that they are not limited to North America. Sightings have been, if anything, even more common in Great Britain, which has no native big cats (except a small and very rare wild cat in Scotland) and very strict laws about what sort of animals can be imported and kept as pets.

Of the many phantom lions of Britain, the one called the Surrey puma is probably the best known. It has been seen on a fairly regular basis in the Surrey district in the south of England since the 1960s. The sightings have been so numerous that they are almost taken for granted. A local newspaper complained about the annual "summer ritual of puma spotting."

What is a typical puma spotting like? On July 19, 1977, London newspapers carried an account of the sighting of a "large grey and lean animal with a small head and 3 ft tail," seen on the grounds of a nursing home at Patchem, near Brighton in Sussex. One man got within forty feet of the lion before it disappeared. As is usual in such cases, a police search of the grounds turned up no material evidence of the creature's existence.

In October that same year near Reigate, Surrey, several workmen claimed to have seen the creature, and one even said he had taken a picture of it. The police were unimpressed. The image on the photo was too small to identify conclusively, though it definitely looked catlike. Police were of the opinion that the animal in the photo was simply a big house cat.

Often the Surrey puma has been described as a large, growling and rather menacing creature. But there is one odd report in which the animal is said to have behaved like—well, a real pussycat. On September 1, 1966, a woman walking through a thistle patch in Hampshire stepped on the tail of what she thought was a puma. The animal reared up on its hind legs and struck out at her with both its paws. The woman then displayed either extraordinary courage or extreme foolhardiness. Instead of running she picked up a stick and hit the beast on the nose. The blow so frightened the poor animal that it clambered up a tree. The woman went for help, but when she returned with others the animal was gone.

The Nottingham lion was first spotted on the morning of July 29, 1976, by two milkmen who were making their rounds near the entrance to the Nottingham airport. They both saw what they were sure was a lion ". . . its head down and its long tail had a bushy end. It was walking slowly away from us."

They watched the beast disappear around the edge of the field and then they called the police. The story made the newspapers and suddenly it seemed everybody in Nottingham was seeing "the lion." There were over sixty sightings reported to police over the next few weeks.

The police checked with all the zoos and private

animal collections within a hundred miles, but no one reported a missing lion. A massive search was carried out using dogs and even a helicopter. At first the police had been quite sympathetic to the lion reports, but as time went on and no evidence turned up, they became more skeptical. Finally official police sources indicated that the whole thing had probably started as a mistake, and the story was being kept alive by attention-seeking journalists and deliberate hoaxes. There is no doubt that the British press, some of which leans heavily toward sensationalism, had a field day with the Nottingham lion.

Is that all there is to it—hysteria and hoax? Well perhaps. Still there have been so many of these reports about strange animals appearing where they shouldn't be, where all reason and logic tells us that they couldn't be, that we begin to wonder.

THE PHANTOM KANGAROO

Phantom hounds can be alarming. Phantom lions are downright frightening. But a phantom kangaroo—that sounds like a joke.

It's no joke. An awful lot of people have reported seeing kangaroos hopping about, in places where there should be no kangaroos—Chicago for example. Real kangaroos live only in Australia and zoos. These phantom kangaroos are said to sometimes be aggressive, even dangerous. Yet after they are sighted, often sighted many times by many different people, no physical trace of them can be found.

There is no clear record of when people first began seeing phantom kangaroos. The tradition isn't an ancient one. One early phantom kangaroo story comes from the small community of South Pittsburg, Tennessee. In January of 1934, according to a newspaper report, the beast was spotted by the Reverend W. J. Handcock, among others. According to the Reverend Handcock, "It was fast as lightning and looked like a giant kangaroo running and leaping across the field."

The same newspaper story tells of a large dog in the area being killed and eaten. Real kangaroos are vegetarians, but the phantom kangaroo was blamed for the killing, and also for the destruction of a large number of chickens. There was no direct evidence linking the phantom kangaroo to the killing of domestic animals, but the kangaroo was blamed anyway. A report of unknown origin speaks of someone having seen the kangaroo carrying a dead sheep or dog under each arm.

An unsuccessful search for the mysterious animal was undertaken, but nothing was found, not even footprints.

In January 1949 a man named Louis Staub was driving at night outside Grove City, Ohio, when he saw something strange hop into the beam of his headlights. "It was about 5½ feet high, hairy and brownish. It had a pointed head. It looked like a kangaroo but it appeared to jump on all fours. I'm certain it wasn't a deer."

Then there was the Minnesota "big-bunny" flap. For several years children in the area of Coon Rapids, Minnesota, reported seeing something that they described as "a very big bunny," a "bunny" that was as tall as they were. One adult, a woman named Barbara Battmer, said that she got a good look at two of these "bunnies" hopping through the woods. She knew they weren't bunnies; they were kangaroos. As is usual in such cases, a search was made but no trace of kangaroos could be found. There were also the usual inquiries to nearby zoos to see if any kangaroos were missing. All zoo kangaroos were present and accounted for.

The most astonishing of all the phantom kangaroo sightings are those that came out of Chicago in 1974. According to the newspapers, early in the morning of October 18, the police on the northwest side of the city received a call from a man who said there was a kangaroo jumping around on his front porch. At first the police didn't take the call too seriously. But the caller was very insistent, so a couple of officers were sent out to investigate.

Much to their surprise the officers found a kangaroo. They chased it, finally cornering the creature in a dark dead-end alley. The kangaroo didn't like being chased and apparently didn't want to be captured either. It began kicking with its big powerful hind legs, which is what kangaroos do when they are on the defensive. The police, who were more puzzled than anything else, didn't want to hurt the kangaroo, so they backed off. The animal then hopped over a fence and disappeared down the street.

During the next few days, a lot of people on the northwest side of Chicago said that they had seen a kangaroo in the neighborhood. A newsboy selling papers on the street corner turned around and saw the kangaroo standing a few feet away from him. "He looked at me, I looked at him, and then he hopped away," the boy said.

The Chicago police got a lot of calls from people who insisted that there was a kangaroo in their backyard rummaging through the garbage cans. Most of these calls were probably the result of mistaken identity—people heard something in the backyard, probably a dog or a cat or a raccoon knocking over the garbage can—but with all the kangaroo hysteria they assumed, or perhaps hoped, that it was the phantom kangaroo they heard. There must have been a fair number of out and out kangaroo hoaxes as well. The newspapers had a lot of fun with such headlines as: KANGAROO STAYS A JUMP AHEAD OF THE POLICE.

Kangaroo sightings then began to spread to towns to the west of Chicago. On November 2, just outside the town of Plano, Illinois, about fifty miles from Chicago, three young men were driving along when:

"We almost ran over it. It jumped onto the road about twenty feet ahead of us . . . it landed on the road near the intersection with the main road, and there was no traffic. It sat up on its haunches . . . and then jumped over a fence about five feet high and disappeared into the woods."

Ten days later in a small Indiana farming community the kangaroo hopped out of a cornfield and up to a drugstore. It was early in the morning and the only witness around was an employee opening up the drugstore:

"I hope some farmer or somebody else sees it or

everybody will think I'm a nut. But it was the kangaroo . . . I know it was." No one else saw it that morning. The mystery beast just hopped down the street and vanished into another cornfield. Other people did report seeing it around the same area over the next few weeks.

By the end of November 1974 the Great Midwestern Kangaroo Flap had died down, but there was another rash of sightings in Illinois the following year and again in 1976. Later waves of phantom-kangaroo sightings have been recorded in Wisconsin, Colorado, Ohio and elsewhere.

When the kangaroo was sighted in Ohio, reporters talked to the director of the Cincinnati Zoo. He said, "We had a kangaroo story about two years ago. I doubt if there's a kangaroo around here on the loose. We never found one. Down the years we've chased after reported black leopards, panthers, and even a polar bear. Anyone seeing the kangaroo, which I doubt exists, should try to keep it in sight and call the zoo."

In case you ever see the phantom kangaroo, that's still pretty good advice.

THE WHITE BIRD OF DOOM

Certain animals or animal spirits have been regarded as omens of doom. That is, they appear when there is about to be a death or some other terrible tragedy. Usually these phantoms are frightening in appearance, like a huge black dog with glowing eyes, or a headless horse. But sometimes the omen can appear in the form of a creature as harmless looking as a white bird.

There is a very old legend from a place called Bala Lake in Wales. At one time the lake did not exist. The dry valley was the site of the castle of a cruel and oppressive prince. The prince had long been tormented by a ghostly voice telling him to stop his evil ways or "Vengeance will come." The prince treated the voice, as he treated most things, with contempt.

The prince had waited many years for the birth of a son and heir. And when his wife finally did have a baby boy, the prince ordered a great celebration at his castle. There was to be a lavish feast, an unending flow of wine with music and dancing that was to go on all night. One of those invited, indeed ordered, to attend and perform at the celebration was an old harper. A harper is a man who sings traditional songs and ballads and accompanies himself on the harp. There are still a few harpers in Wales today, but centuries ago the harper was considered an essential part of every major celebration.

The harper in this particular account was well known, but quite elderly. After several hours of playing and singing he was worn out and found a quiet corner in which to rest.

As he sat there trying to recover his strength, he heard a voice whisper in his ear, "Vengeance, vengeance!"

When he turned to see who was talking to him, he was astonished to discover it was a small white bird. The bird hovered near him, and then began to fly slowly toward the door. Somehow the harper knew that he was being asked to follow. He did so immediately, without even bothering to take his harp. The bird led the old man beyond the castle walls. Every few moments he could hear the cry "Vengeance, vengeance!" The bird led him across the moors, which could be extremely dangerous, particularly at night. In some mysterious way the bird seemed to know the safest path. The farther they went the louder and more insistent came the cries of "Vengeance, vengeance!"

Finally, when they reached the top of a hill over-looking the valley, the old harper was too exhausted to go on. He stopped to rest. At this point the bird disappeared. There were no more cries of "Vengeance!" All the harper could hear was what sounded like the loud murmur of a rushing brook.

The old man suddenly realized he had done a foolish and dangerous thing. The prince would be furious when he found out the harper had left the celebration without permission. Everyone feared the prince's anger. But there was nothing to be done about it. The old man knew he would never be able to find his way back through the moors to the castle in the dark. He would have to await daylight, and the prince's rage.

The exhausted harper fell asleep. When he awoke the sun was already up and revealed an astonishing sight. The valley where the castle had once stood was now a lake. During the night it had been completely flooded. And there, floating on the surface of the lake, was the old man's harp.

The Oxenhams, an old English family originally from Devonshire, have been tormented for centuries by a white bird which is an omen of death.

The first recorded instance of the appearance of the white bird of the Oxenhams was in September 1635. James Oxenham, a robust and vigorous young man, was suddenly and mysteriously taken ill. No one seemed to know what was wrong with James but it was assumed that because of his youth and strength he would recover. Then on September 3 a white bird was seen hovering over his bed. Two days later James Oxenham was dead.

Within a few days James Oxenham's wife, his infant daughter and his wife's young sister all died mysteriously. In each case the white bird had been seen hovering about them shortly before death. Other members of the family and of the household staff had been stricken with the mysterious ailment, but the white bird was only seen near those who actually died.

In 1820, nearly two hundred years later, an elderly member of the Oxenham family lay dying at his home in Sidmouth. The servants who attended the dying man swore that they had seen a white bird fly in the door, dart across the bed in which their master lay, and disappear in one of the drawers of the bureau. When they searched the drawers, they could find no sign of the bird.

In December of 1873 G. N. Oxenham who lived in London was sitting in the dining room of his home with his daughter and a friend of the family. They heard some shouting outside. When they looked out the window, they saw a large white bird perched in a tree near the window. Some workmen apparently were trying to scare the bird away by shouting at it. But the bird just sat there for several minutes. Within a week Oxenham became ill and died. A nurse who was with him during his final hours reported hearing the fluttering of a bird's wings in the man's room.

Unquestionably the most famous and tragic event connected with the Oxenham family's white bird took place at the wedding of Lady Margaret Oxenham, in the early eighteenth century.

Her father, Sir James Oxenham of Devon, had invited a large number of guests to a feast on the night before the marriage was to take place. Sir James, who was in a jolly and expansive mood, was making a speech to the assembled guests when suddenly he turned pale and was unable to utter a word for a few moments. He recovered enough to be able to finish his speech, but it was clear that he had received a terrible shock.

All the guests knew that something had frightened him, but Sir James insisted that all was normal, and that the guests should go on enjoying themselves. Only after the banquet was over did the nobleman confide to a trusted servant what had happened. While he was speaking, he had seen a white bird appear from nowhere, fly toward his daughter Margaret, circle her several times, and then disappear. No one else in the room had been able to see the bird. The servant, who had been with the Oxenham family for many years, knew the legend of the white bird. He tried to reassure Sir James that the white bird was nothing more than an old wives' tale, and that his daughter was in no danger. But Sir James could not be consoled, and in truth the servant didn't believe his own reassuring words.

The next morning, just as the marriage service began, a man who had been hiding near the altar of the church jumped out and stabbed the bride through the heart. He then stabbed himself to death with the same knife. The murderer was a suitor who had been rejected by the Oxenham family.

CHAPTER

8

GHOSTLY
PETS

For many people a pet dog or cat or other animal is an integral part of the family, as much loved as any human relative. It's no wonder, therefore, that there have been many accounts of people who have seen, heard or otherwise experienced the presence of a pet who has just died.

One of the best known of all the ghost pet accounts concerns the writer Albert Payson Terhune. In the early years of the twentieth century, Terhune was America's leading writer of dog stories. It seemed that everyone had read at least one of his books. In addition to writing about dogs, Terhune was a real dog lover and he had a lot of them on the farm where he lived and worked. Terhune was best known for his stories about collies, and many of the dogs he owned were collies, but he loved all kinds of dogs. One of his favorites was a large, fawn-colored, short-haired dog of mixed ancestry, named Rex. Rex's appearance was unmistakable because he had a large scar on his face. Often when the Terhune family sat down to dinner, Rex would come to the window and stare in. The dog also spent a lot of time in the hallway sprawled out next to the author's study.

Rex was killed by a car in 1916. A short time later an old friend of the Terhune family, the Reverend Appleton Grannis, came to stay at the Terhune home. The Reverend Grannis had not seen the Terhunes in years and had never seen Rex and knew nothing about him.

Terhune and the Reverend Grannis were sitting in the dining room talking when Grannis suddenly said that he saw a strange dog looking in at the window. Terhune turned, but the dog disappeared. Grannis said that the animal at the window did not look like any of the dogs he had seen on the Terhune farm and he described it. The description matched Rex perfectly, down to the scar on the face.

Two years after Rex's death, another friend of the author's family, Henry A. Healy, insisted he had seen the figure of Rex lying at his feet when he visited the Terhune farm.

Terhune himself never saw Rex's ghost but he noticed that for years after Rex's death another one of his dogs refused to walk over a spot that had been favored by the dead dog.

A fairly typical case was reported by Mrs. Joy Baterski. She said that Red, the family Irish setter, had died on August 26, 1965. The animal had been the family pet for over fourteen years and was greatly missed. Red was buried in the backyard.

On the night after Red's death and burial, Mrs. Baterski was awakened by what she was sure was Red's barking. Though many dog owners can recognize their own pet's bark, Red had an unusual and very distinctive bark. Mrs. Baterski described him as sounding like a "hoarse seal." She insisted that his bark could not be mistaken for that of any other dog. Her husband was also awakened by the sounds. These mysterious barkings continued off and on for several weeks, until the Baterskis got a new dog, a German shepherd puppy. "From that day forward," she said, "the mysterious barking was heard no more."

Mrs. Baterski described her experience in a letter to Raymond Bayless, a researcher and writer of ghostly occurrences:

"The last and final time [the barking was heard was] almost a week later, when I was crying in my sleep, and my husband woke me. Only I heard the barking then. It was becoming more distant. At this point I was so upset that I even insisted that my husband dig the dog up to make certain that he was dead. My husband assured me that he was.

"Who can say if we had not brought another dog into the house whether or not the phenomenon might have continued?

"I would say that within a period of about four weeks we were awakened by Red's barking at least five times and at least once a week. But the last time only I heard it."

Bayless got a statement from Mr. Lawrence Baterski which confirmed his wife's account in every detail. A neighbor of the Baterskis also wrote Bayless. "Red had the most unusual bark I have ever heard and it could not be mistaken. After hearing the dog over thirteen years they [the Baterskis] would surely recognize the bark."

Al H. Morrison of New York supplied Bayless with a very similar story. Late on Sunday afternoon in June of 1956, the dog that he had lived with for fourteen years died. Morrison's letter continues:

"In late August of the same year at the same time of day—2 P.M. or so on Sunday—I had a new client sitting there when there came a loud happy barking from my dog. You don't live with a dog for fourteen years and fail to recognize its voice.

"I would have written it all off as my own wishful thinking but my client heard it at the same time. It was so loud that it frightened her, and she asked, 'Where is the dog?' I thought about it and decided that she couldn't deal with such a story so I just said, 'Oh she's around here somewhere' and went on working."

Morrison said that he doubted if the incident would recur. "It seemed to me that it took an enormous effort and energy to get back through, and that she wouldn't have the energy again."

Another of Bayless's cases comes from Australia. It

was related by a man named William A. Courtney. In 1953 Courtney was living in the small town of Sarina in northern Australia. He had a valuable greyhound named Lady to which he was very much attached. But the dog became ill and died suddenly.

"That night I lay on my bed thinking of her and grieving when I suddenly heard pattering footsteps coming along the passage from the front door. . . . The footsteps entered my room beside my bed.

"I sprang up and turned on the light fully expecting to see Lady stretched on the floor. But the room was empty, or at least I saw nothing."

Courtney couldn't find anything unusual in the house or yard to account for the noise. Then he realized that he had heard the sounds at 10 P.M., the hour when Lady had usually come in for the night.

A somewhat older account was found in a journal devoted to ghosts and other psychic matters. Mrs. W.E. Dickson told how her dog, Butch, died at about noon on Tuesday, March 29, 1949.

That night she thought she heard Butch whining and crying. At first she didn't want to tell her husband about what she heard because she was afraid that he would not believe her. In the morning he said, "I don't know if you will believe this, but I heard Butch crying all night." They decided not to tell anyone else, but one of their neighbors reported dreaming that she heard Butch. The strange whinings and barkings continued for about three months.

Mrs. Dickson added, "And another unusual thing

happened about two mornings after he died—I was positive I saw a shadow jump up on the bed where my husband was lying. I cannot define this in any other way except as a shadow."

At an old Victorian house in the town of Midland Park, New Jersey, occupants and visitors have seen or otherwise experienced the spirit of a cat—usually described as a small yellow and white animal.

One of the house's former owners, a painter named Ethelyn Woodlock, had reported seeing several ghosts in the house. Her favorite was always the cat. It stayed mainly in a small third-floor bedroom. While she lived in the house, Mrs. Woodlock changed the beds in the room four times. That didn't seem to disturb the cat ghost in the least. He, or she, no one knows for sure, seemed equally comfortable on any of the beds. Indeed, people who never actually saw the ghost cat would often find a warm spot on the bed where the comforter had been pushed down. It was as if a cat that had been curled up asleep on that very spot had just awakened and left.

Mrs. Woodlock left the house in 1979, and the new owners never reported seeing most of the ghosts that she said were there. The cat, however, remained a familiar presence in the small third-floor bedroom.

Hundreds, possibly thousands of similar accounts of ghostly pets have been told by people all over the world. In many respects they resemble the stories told by people who believe they have seen or otherwise experienced the spirit of a recently dead relative or friend. One important difference is that none of the stories that I know of indicates that the ghostly pet has come back as a frightening or evil force, as is sometimes the case with human ghosts.

Are all of these tales the result of mistakes and wishful thinking? Well perhaps, but sometimes one wonders, and hopes.

ANIMAL POLTER- GEISTS

The word poltergeist is German. It means noisy spirit. When people say a house or some other place has a poltergeist it usually means that there are lots of strange and unexplainable noises. Objects may be moved or even thrown around. Most of the time people don't see ghosts or phantoms or apparitions, or whatever you want to call them. But occasionally poltergeist cases have involved ghostly animals, usually strange and unnatural looking ones.

One of the best-known cases of this type took place in the nineteenth century in England at a place called Willington Mill. The mill was owned by the Proctor family. For over ten years it was the scene of all manner of poltergeist disruptions. There were loud and dreadful noises, sometimes sounding like a galloping horse or donkey and at other times like falling metal tools. Doors creaked and opened mysteriously. Piles of wood began to emit crackling sounds, as if they were burning when they weren't. At times the sound of loud rapping was almost constant. But worst of all were the apparitions in human or animal or animal-like shape.

A memorable experience at Willington Mill was related by a man named Thomas Davidson. He was courting a maid in the Proctor household. One evening Davidson was standing by the mill when what looked like a whitish cat came out to him. Davidson was apparently no animal lover, for his first reaction was to try and kick the creature. When he did, his boot went right through the form as if it wasn't there at all. The cat, or whatever it was, then disappeared. It reappeared a few minutes later, hopping like a rabbit. Davidson aimed another kick at it, but once again, his boot passed right through the shape. The third time it appeared it was large as a sheep and it glowed in the dark. By this time Thomas Davidson was a badly frightened man.

According to an account written by his son:

"All muscle power seemed for the moment paralyzed. It moved on, disappearing at the same spot as the preceding apparition. My father declared if it was possible for 'hair to stand on end' his did just then. Thinking for once that he had seen enough, he went home, and it was a long time before he told anyone about what he had seen."

A man named Wedgewood reported that he had seen a tabby cat in the furnace room of the mill. There was nothing unusual about the cat's appearance. But instead of walking like an ordinary cat, it wriggled along the ground like a snake. He tried to follow it, but it passed through a solid stone wall.

One woman was standing in the kitchen when she heard a dog bark; then she felt what seemed to be paws land heavily on her shoulders. There was, of course, no dog to be seen. Children in the area sometimes reported seeing what they described as a "funny cat or bonny monkey" during the years of the disturbances at the mill.

Ultimately the strange noises, and the strange sights just faded away without any real explanation.

A more recent American poltergeist case took place in southern California in the 1930s. The scene was the home of a Mrs. James H. Rogers. All of the family heard strange noises including clicking and what sounded like footsteps.

One night Mrs. Rogers's daughter was awakened by noises coming from the kitchen. When she went to investigate, she was able to find nothing out of the ordinary. When she returned to her bedroom, she saw a strange dog there. The animal stared fixedly at her. She became aware there was something very unusual about this dog—it was semitransparent. She could see through it. As she walked toward the dog waving her hand, the figure vanished.

When Sara Joyce moved into part of an old commercial building in the center of Genessee, Ohio, in

1974, she began to hear all sorts of strange noises. There were the unexplained footsteps, the sounds of doors opening and closing. All and all it was fairly typical poltergeist activity. One night, said Mrs. Joyce, there was "the most tremendous racket . . . a huge, noisy, rushing racket going on, like someone shoving furniture or heavy equipment back and forth across the room." The noises became so bad that the police were called. As often happens in such cases, the noise stopped shortly before the police arrived, and started up again just after they left.

There were a few apparitions. There was the semi-transparent figure of an old man who threw something at Mrs. Joyce. His eyes seemed to say, "Do you see me? Do you see me?" She screamed at him, "I see you," after which he faded away.

But the most alarming apparition connected with this burst of poltergeist activity was not human. Here is how Mrs. Joyce described it in a letter to Arthur Myers, author of *The Ghostly Register*:

"One morning early, I came down the stairs, turned the corner into the kitchen doorway, and quick as lightning something jumped onto my arm. It was a rat! A huge, silvery, shiny, golden, transparent rat! It had an abundance of hair, and I felt its claws on my skin as it climbed up my arm. When I screamed it disappeared. I stood on the spot several minutes in disbelief. How could this have been? I began to doubt whether I had really seen it, looking at my arm to see if there were marks on my skin.

There were no visual marks, but I could still feel the sensation of claws pricking my skin."

Some years later, when Sara Joyce's son was re-modeling the old building, he found the dried out remains of a huge rat under the floorboards in the kitchen.

Lawrence D. Copeland reported that his house in Hingham, Massachusetts, was troubled by poltergeist activity. It wasn't a gloomy old mansion, but rather a cheerful colonial reproduction built in 1966.

Among the many strange and unexplainable sounds was one of a cat climbing up a screen. Visitors would sometimes ask, "Why don't you let the cat in? I hear the poor thing clawing at the screen."

The trouble was all Copeland's cats were safely in-side, and there were no screens!

Copeland has said, "We did not intend to live in a haunted house (and we don't really think that we do now) but we are very puzzled."

THE DOG
ON THE
STAIRS

Margaret duPont Lee was a very wealthy lady who spent many years doing charitable work and collecting ghost stories about the state of Virginia, in which she lived. During the 1930s she published two books on Virginia ghosts. Most of her stories are about the ghosts that have been seen in the state's old mansions and plantations, or that have been connected in one way or another with the state's old and prominent families. Her accounts usually contain names, dates and places. But there is a curious story in Mrs. Lee's collection that has none of this supporting information. It is therefore worthless as evidence for the existence of ghosts. However, it does have a ghost dog.

The unnamed narrator of the story, who was a young woman, seems to have rented rooms in what was once a large private home. The widow of the man who owned the house and one of her daughters had converted the old family home into a boarding house.

The narrator was returning home from work one hot summer afternoon. "I started upstairs to my bedroom and on crossing the landing, midway, I saw a large black dog lying on the steps beyond it and just opposite the rear door that led to the south window. He was apparently asleep and as a refreshing breeze was blowing in I thought he had selected this place for his afternoon nap because of its cool shadiness, especially as the second-floor hall was but dimly lighted so I was not much surprised when he refused to move or even to open his eyes and notice me when I spoke to him. I again asked him kindly to move and again he refused to notice me. The third time, however, I spoke quite loudly, ordering him to get up and let me pass. Then a strange thing happened that startled me very much. Without rising or moving his head or limbs, and continuing to lie on his side with his eyes closed, he glided up the steps and along the hall until he reached the far end then, without a door being opened, disappeared."

The next night exactly the same thing happened. "The dog was lying in exactly the same spot and disappeared when I stamped my foot at him."

The narrator was very busy on those days, and so didn't have time to question the owner of the house about this strange and ghostly dog.

The third night was much cooler and the phantom dog did not appear at the spot on the landing. The narrator, however, was expecting a visit from a friend. When the doorbell rang, she went down the steps to greet her visitor. "When I got to the place where the dog had lain I felt something jerk my arm violently and I jumped as if I had been shot." She looked all around, but there was nothing in sight except her friend, who was coming up the stairs.

Later, as her friend was leaving, something awful happened. The visitor reached the spot where the dog had been and took a sudden and unexpected fall. She struck her head on the hardwood floor. "She suffered with violent headaches for three months and died from the effects of that fall."

The dog never appeared again, but a few days after the narrator saw it for the last time another friend came to visit. The two spent the evening playing checkers. During the game the narrator became very thirsty and got up to get a drink from a water cooler that was in the hall just outside the door.

"I opened the door and started back with a loud cry, for in the very doorway stood the full-length black, shadowy form of a man. My friend ran to me and as she came the figure moved back into the dark part of the hall and disappeared just as the dog had done, without moving its head or limbs."

That did it! The narrator was now thoroughly frightened and determined to move out. "I had a beautiful room with a pleasant family and hated to move." But first there had been a phantom dog, and now this dark and ghostly form. Enough was enough.

The very next day the narrator told her landlady that she was going to move, and why. The landlady was saddened but not really surprised. She said others had seen the apparitions. The shadowy figure of the man appeared to be her late husband, and the dog was his pet dog that had the habit of sleeping on the stairs in that spot on warm days. The landlady said the ghostly figures had never attempted to frighten or hurt anyone, but just seemed to want to be in the old and familiar family house.

The landlady then asked if the narrator had seen the figure of a young woman. "When I said 'No,' she replied it was her daughter who often appeared to them, and added that if I were to remain she would appear to me. I moved that day . . ."

THE
ROARING
BULL

In some parts of the world people believe that after death the spirit may return in a different form, sometimes the form of an animal. This sort of belief has never taken hold in the West. However, there are a few stories of the dead, usually an evil person, returning in the form of an animal.

In the county of Shropshire in England, farmers delighted in repeating the tale of the Roaring Bull of Bagbury.

It was said that the owner of a place called Bagbury Farm had lived a very evil life. Indeed, people could recall only two good deeds that he had ever done. Once he gave a piece of clothing to a poor man, and another time he gave a piece of bread and cheese to a half-starved village lad. That was not much to weigh against all the bad things that he had done in his lifetime.

When he died he was not widely mourned by his

neighbors but his spirit refused to rest. He returned to his farm, not in human shape but in the form of a bull that roared and raged until the shutters flew open and shingles were thrown from the roofs.

The roaring began about nine every evening and went on all night. It was quite impossible for anyone in the vicinity to get any sleep with that sort of racket going on. So the people sent for twelve parsons. They were to "lay the ghost"—that is shrink it down to a manageable size, trap it, and then get rid of it. "Laying a ghost" is a form of exorcism.

The parsons found the ghostly bull was very powerful. They were able to drive it off the farm and into Hessington Church. Once inside the church the bull roared and stomped, and made an attempt to get past the parsons who were guarding the door. The bull actually cracked the wall of the church from top to bottom. It is said that even today local residents will show visitors the crack in the wall made by the Roaring Bull.

Finally through prayers and threats the twelve parsons were able to shrink the bull down to a tiny size and put it in a snuffbox. The ghost begged that the snuffbox be thrown into the river near Bagbury Bridge. He boasted that every mare that passed over the bridge would lose her foal and every woman would lose her child. Obviously the parsons weren't going to allow that to happen. According to the legend the snuffbox with the ghost inside was shipped off to the Holy Land and thrown into the Red Sea.

Still a lot of villagers were not entirely convinced that the matter had been fully settled. They were very wary about crossing Bagbury Bridge, particularly at night.

Lady Howard, who lived in the reign of King James I (1603–1625), was famous both for her beauty and her cruelty. She was cruel to her only daughter and to her four husbands, all of whom died under unexplained circumstances.

Local legend has it that after she died, Lady Howard was forced to do penance for her sins. She returned to earth in the form of a ghostly hound. Every night she is forced to run many miles from her home at Fitzford to Okehampton Park, where she picks up a single blade of grass in her mouth and then runs back to her old home. This penance is to continue until all the grass has been removed from Okehampton. At the rate of one blade of grass a night, she still has centuries of work ahead of her.

A whole host of strange tales have grown up around the very eccentric Miss Beswick who lived in a mansion called Birchen Bower in Hollinwood near the city of Manchester in the midlands of England. She died around the year 1770. During her lifetime Miss Beswick developed an obsessive fear of being buried alive. She left a lot of money to her doctor on the condition that he keep her body out of the ground after she died. It seems that he embalmed the body with tar, wrapped it up like a mummy, leaving the face exposed and gave it to the Manchester Natural History Society, where it attracted a lot of curious attention for nearly a century. After about one hundred years the trustees of the society decided the exhibit was too gruesome. So on August 15, 1868, the remains of the strange lady were finally buried. By this time she was most certainly dead.

There was another curious provision in Miss Beswick's will. Every twenty-one years her body was to be taken back to Birchen Bower and left there for one week. It was usually housed in the granary of the old farm. On the day the body was to be removed all the horses and cows were found to have been turned loose. Sometimes a cow would be found up in the hayloft, though how it got there was always a mystery. It was assumed that the strange old lady's ghost was playing some sort of joke.

In addition to putting cows in haylofts, Miss Beswick's ghost was also believed to appear in the form of a cow or other animal. Still another tradition about Miss Beswick was that she had hidden a vast sum of money somewhere on her estate.

These ghostly animals are seen between the old barn and the horse pool. Some people think that

Miss Beswick buried her treasure in that area and would be willing to point it out to anyone brave enough to go up to her—in whatever form she appears—and simply ask her about it.

So far, no one has been that brave. And the treasure, if there ever was one, remains hidden.

THE WHITE
RABBIT
OF CRANK

In the early seventeenth century, during the reign of James I of England, witchcraft was considered a serious business. Merely being accused of witchcraft might result in arrest, trial and punishment—often death. The story of the White Rabbit of Crank goes back to that superstitious and violent time.

Anyone might be suspected of witchcraft. But old women who were poor and lived on the fringes of society were particularly vulnerable. In the tiny village of Crank, in the county of Lancashire, there lived such an old woman. She was a foreigner, though no one seemed sure where she had originally come from. She lived in a little cottage alone, except for her granddaughter, a girl named Jenny. The old woman made a small living by concocting herbal remedies, which she sold to the villagers. Though the only potions she was known to have sold were medicinal, there were rumors that she also made poisons and engaged in other black arts—that in fact she was a witch. Most people in the village stayed away from her cottage unless they needed one of her remedies.

Also living in the village at the time was a rather repulsive character named Pullen, who was known to be both violent and miserly. When he came down with a seemingly fatal and incurable disease, he went to the old woman for one of her medicines. Though he paid what he considered an enormous amount of money for the potion, it didn't help. In fact, his condition actually seemed to get worse. Pullen became convinced that not only had the old woman cheated him, she was actually trying to poison him with one of her witch's brews.

According to a popular belief of the time, the best way to break a witch's spell was to bleed the witch to death. Pullen enlisted the aid of a fellow in the village whose character was, if anything, worse than his own. Dick Piers, who made his living as a poacher, had actually been thrown out of the army because of his bad character. In those days the British army was filled with criminal types—and to be thrown out was an unusual and dubious distinction.

One night Pullen and Piers put on disguises and set out for the old woman's cottage. She was asleep when the two burst in. They dragged her from her bed, and cut her arm, causing a gush of blood. The old woman cried out, and her granddaughter, Jenny, who had been sleeping in the next room, awoke. She was badly frightened and grabbed her beloved pet rabbit for comfort. It was a very large white rabbit with drooping ears. Clutching the rabbit, she went into her grandmother's room and saw the two men. They saw her too. Still holding the rabbit tightly, Jenny turned and ran out of the house, with Pullen and Piers in hot pursuit. She disappeared over the crest of a hill, and when her pursuers got to the top they found only the rabbit. Swearing, Piers killed the poor animal with a single kick. By that time, however, the girl was gone. Pullen and Piers decided that now that there was a witness they had better not try and return to the old woman's cottage.

While they abandoned their plan to murder the woman they believed to be a witch, they still were responsible for a death. When Jenny ran from the cottage in terror, she fell into a ditch and hit her head. The next day a farmer found her frozen body.

The only person who could possibly connect Pullen and Piers with the girl's death was the old woman. And though she suspected who the assailants were, she could not clearly identify them since they had been in disguise. Besides, few in the village would have been willing to take the word of a woman who was generally thought to be a witch, and a foreigner to boot. No matter how vile their reputations, Pullen and Piers were local men. After poor Jenny's funeral, the old woman moved from the village forever.

There the matter would have ended, were it not for the white rabbit. Dick Piers was making his way home one day when he saw a white rabbit hopping across the fields. White rabbits were not common in the seventeenth century. Indeed, Jenny's pet was the only white rabbit that most of the people of the village of Crank had ever seen. Piers was absolutely certain that what he saw was the ghost of the rabbit he had killed just a few days earlier. He ran home and locked the door behind him. He was able to shut the rabbit out of his house, but not out of his mind. He began to avoid going out for fear of seeing the creature. The rabbit and the crime connected with it began to weigh heavily on his mind. After a few weeks he could take it no more. He described what he had done to some of his friends. The following morning he was found at the bottom of the local quarry. He had either jumped or fallen in, perhaps while running away from something.

With one witness against him moved away and the other dead, Pullen felt safe. But his health continued to decline. He became more sullen and miserable by the day. One night while he happened to be passing the old woman's cottage, he looked down and saw a large white rabbit hopping alongside him. The sight panicked him. He ran, but the rabbit ran too, easily keeping pace. When he stopped, the rabbit stopped. Terrified and desperate, Pullen took off across the open fields toward his home, with the rabbit matching him stride for stride. A few yards from his home he collapsed with fright and exhaustion. His neighbors found him an hour or so later and took him inside. Pullen lingered for about a week raving about the white rabbit before he finally died.

Even today people in the area say that "the White Rabbit of Crank" can be seen on dark nights. It's considered very bad luck to catch a glimpse of this particular phantom.

THE TERROR OF LE GEVADUAN

Throughout history there have been many tales of werewolves. Most of these tales are legends—stories that have little or no basis in fact—though people may have believed them. A few of history's werewolves were murderous madmen, who thought themselves to be wild animals and tore their victims apart. Then there are the events that terrorized a section of France known as Le Gevaduan for three years beginning in 1754.

In the rugged mountains surrounding the village of Saint Etienne de Lugdares, children were often sent out to watch the sheep and cattle grazing in isolated summer pastures. In mid July 1764 the body of a young girl was found in one of the valleys. Her heart had been torn out. This was the first recorded killing in the reign of terror by a creature that came to be known as the Beast of Le Gevaduan. Within a few days there were several more killings of children reported.

The killings spread panic among the peasants. They gathered in their children and left the livestock to fend for itself. But a few weeks passed without any additional killings, and life seemed to return to normal.

Then, late in August, a peasant woman from the village of Langogne reported that she had seen a fantastic creature. It walked on two legs like a man, but it was covered with short reddish hair and had a piglike snout. It was as big as a donkey and had rather short ears and a long tail. The woman said that the creature had frightened off her dogs, but had itself been frightened by her cattle, which attacked it with lowered horns.

The description sounded so fantastic that even the most superstitious among the peasants laughed at it. They stopped laughing within a few days, however, when the monster was reported again. This time the witness was Jean-Pierre Pourcher, a man known for his courage and truthfulness. Pourcher fired at the creature with his musket, but either the shot missed or the creature was unaffected by the bullet.

And the murders of children began again. Many who had been taken out of isolated pastures after the first alarm had been allowed to return. Now some of them fell victim to a creature that killed and mutilated. Not surprisingly, rumors began to circulate that the region was afflicted by a *loup-garou,* as the werewolf is called in France.

Word of the murders in Le Gevaduan reached the king. He dispatched a company of soldiers to deal with the beast. The soldiers arrived in February 1765. Almost immediately they encountered the creature— or something. They opened fire on it, but it ran off into the underbrush and could not be located. There were no more killings for a few weeks. The soldiers assumed that they had mortally wounded the beast, and that it had crawled off to some hidden place to die. They returned to the palace at Versailles to report to the king that they had successfully completed their mission. The report was premature.

As the weather warmed up and the children were again sent to the mountains to tend cattle and sheep, the killings started all over again. The king received another urgent appeal, but this time he was slow to respond. It wasn't until early in 1766 that a second military expedition was sent to the area. The soldiers killed a large wolf which they confidently declared to be "the Beast of Le Gevaduan." They marched back to Versailles in triumph, and once again the king declared the emergency was over. And once again he was wrong.

The beast continued to stalk Le Gevaduan, and several villages were actually abandoned because of fear of the monster. Finally in June 1767, nearly three years after the killings had begun, a local nobleman organized a huge party of hunters and swore that they would not rest until the monster really had been killed.

On June 19 the beast was surrounded in a patch of woods at Le Sogne d'Auvert. One of the hunters, Jean Chastel, had a gun loaded with silver bullets. According to tradition, only a silver bullet can kill a werewolf. When he saw the beast he fired two shots. The second struck the monster in the heart and it fell dead.

The carcass was then carried from village to village as proof that the terrible beast finally was really dead. Unfortunately, the accounts are not clear as to just exactly what the thing looked like. Most descriptions make it sound like a very large but strange-looking wolf, with close cropped ears and unusual hoof-like feet.

In the warm June weather the carcass soon began to rot, and it had to be buried. While no one seems to know where the remains of the monster were buried, tourists are still shown the spot where Jean Chastel is supposed to have felled it. His gun can be seen in the church at Saint Martin-de-Bouchaux.

What was the Beast of Le Gevaduan? Some believe that it was just a large and exceptionally ferocious wolf, or perhaps several wolves whose killings were all attributed to a single creature by the frightened peasants. The peasants may also have exaggerated the extent and nature of the killings, attributing unrelated deaths to the beast.

One theory holds that there was an outbreak of rabies among the wolves of Le Gevaduan, and that the disease is what caused them to behave in so vicious and uncharacteristic a manner. Normally wolves avoid human beings.

Others say the beast was really a man—a homicidal madman who was never really caught but died at about the same time Chastel shot the wolf.

And then there are those who think that the Beast of Le Gevaduan was exactly what the peasants thought it was, the *loup-garou*—the werewolf.

In any event, this is among the most intriguing and best documented of all werewolf accounts.

THE TIGER
AND
THE LEPER

Leprosy is a horrible, disfiguring disease. Today there are effective treatments, and it is no longer the scourge it was once. But for centuries leprosy was one of the most feared diseases. Lepers—people afflicted with the disease—were often locked away in special camps or colonies. If they were not sent away they were shunned by others, even members of their own families. People feared that if they got too close to a leper they too might catch the disease, though it is not highly infectious. As the disease progressed, those afflicted became terrible to look at. Lepers were more often hated and feared than they were pitied. They became objects of almost supernatural dread.

By the early years of the twentieth century the fear of leprosy had declined greatly in Europe (the disease had never been very common in America). But in places like India it was still a scourge—and the object of supernatural dread.

Another object of nearly supernatural dread in India was the tiger. Today the tiger is an endangered species that has nearly been wiped out over much of its range. But it is still the largest, and potentially most dangerous, of the big cats. Normally the tiger avoids contact with humans. But occasionally a tiger will turn into a man eater. This usually happens to tigers that are old or have been ill or injured, so that they are no longer swift and agile enough to catch their prey. For such tigers human beings are an easier kill. Small wonder that unarmed and unprotected villagers might come to regard a particularly dangerous tiger as some sort of supernatural beast.

These twin fears—leprosy and tigers—came together in a story told by a Colonel De Silva, a British army officer who spent many years in India during the early part of this century.

Colonel De Silva told of how he saw an enormous tiger attack an old man stricken with leprosy. De Silva was unable to do anything to help the old man. Before dying the old leper cursed De Silva and his family for not coming to his aid.

About a year later rumors of another man-eating tiger spread throughout the district. This tiger, it was said, was not a normal yellow, but rather a ghostly white. Stranger still was the fact that those who had only been wounded by the tiger almost immediately developed leprosy. Some of the villagers began to say that the ghostly tiger was somehow in league with the spirit of the dead leper.

De Silva saw the ghostly tiger once when he was alone. He fired at it but missed and the animal ran off into the darkness. He saw it again a few nights later. But this time it was stalking the colonel's wife, child and the child's nurse. "I must fire at all costs," De Silva recalled thinking. "If mortal, I must kill it; if ghostly, the noise of my rifle might make it disappear." He had very little time to reflect, for the big cat sprang at the three terrified people. De Silva shot, and the animal simply disappeared. But it was too late. The nurse died of shock almost immediately. De Silva's little boy received a scratch on the cheek from the tiger's claw. A short time later he developed a particularly virulent case of leprosy and died from it.

After that the white tiger was never seen again. Was it all coincidence, or was the old leper's curse fulfilled?

THE RATS
OF
THE RHINE

Surely you have heard the story of the Pied Piper
of Hamelin. He rid the German town of Hamelin of
rats. Then when he was not paid for his services he
led the children of the city away as well. In one version of the tale the character was a rat catcher, a sort
of medieval exterminator.

Today rats are a nuisance, and sometimes worse.
But in medieval Europe rats were a constant and very
serious threat. They spread disease, and they destroyed food. When food stocks were already low rats
could bring on a famine. That is why there are many
legends about the nearly supernatural power of rats.
Here is one of the grimmest of them.

One year the usually rich provinces of the Rhine
Valley in Germany were struck by terrible rain and
hailstorms. The wheat in the fields, which was ready
for harvest, was broken and rotted quickly on the

damp earth. Soon the poor had exhausted their limited reserves of food and faced starvation.

The most powerful and richest man in the stricken region was Bishop Hatto of Mantz. Despite his title the bishop was a far from godly man. He ruled the region like a tyrant, acquiring not only great power but great wealth. He was cruel and arrogant. While the poor went hungry, Bishop Hatto's own personal storehouses were well stocked with grain.

Finally the people appealed to the bishop to give them food. After a week they received his response. His messenger told the people that all those who did not have the means to pay for food should gather in front of the great barn on his estate that afternoon.

So it was that a large crowd of the starving poor appeared in front of the great barn. At the appointed time grim-faced soldiers threw open the doors to the barn and the crowd surged inside. It was dark, and at first they could see nothing. But it didn't take long to discover that instead of a barn filled with sacks of grain for the taking, this barn was completely empty. Before the disappointment and shock really set in, the soldiers closed the heavy doors of the barn, trapping the crowd inside.

The true horror of their situation dawned on people only when they began to smell smoke and hear the crackling of flames. The bishop's men had set fire to the barn. All of those trapped inside were killed.

Bishop Hatto reasoned that he did not have

enough grain to feed all the starving people, and that they would probably have died anyway. In the meantime they would have become a dangerous and rebellious rabble, who might well have robbed him of his own stocks of food, which would have only prolonged their miserable lives for a few extra days or weeks. It was a hard decision, the bishop thought, but powerful men often have to make hard decisions.

So it was a relatively untroubled Bishop Hatto who went to sleep on the night of the massacre. And it was a well-rested and placid Bishop Hatto who ate breakfast the next morning. But his serenity was soon to be shattered. As he entered the great hall of the Bishop's Palace, he saw that his own recently painted portrait was now in shreds. Who could have committed such an outrage? When the bishop approached the tattered picture, several large rats jumped out from behind the frame. It was the rats that had destroyed the canvas.

That was just the beginning. Messengers told Hatto that a horde of hungry rats had descended upon the area, destroying his fields and all of the grain that he had stored in his warehouses.

From the window of his palace Hatto could see an army of the rodents moving toward his palace. They were already close enough for him to hear their high-pitched squeaking. The rats that had destroyed his portrait were only an advance guard—scouts for the invasion to come.

Though terrified by the sight Hatto was a man of action, and he formed a plan. On a small island in the middle of the Rhine was a stone tower. Hatto had occasionally used the tower as a summer retreat. Here, he reasoned, he would be safe from the marauding rats.

He snuck out of his palace by a back exit and followed a path down to the river. A waiting boatman took him to the island. The bishop wasted no time scrambling to the top room in the tower and locking the door. Then he collapsed in near exhaustion.

He did not rest for long. Soon the sound of the squeaking and scrambling of thousands of rats reached his ears. Unwillingly he looked out the window. The rats were there. Wave after wave of them was swimming across the river to the island.

At first the rat army paused at the foot of the sheer stone tower, and the bishop had a moment of hope, but only a moment. Rats began scrambling up the tower walls, finding secure holds for their tiny claws in the rough stone. They reached the top of the tower and began pouring in through the windows.

Hours later some of the bishop's servants made their way to the top of the tower. All that remained of the once mighty Bishop Hatto was a skeleton picked clean of all of its flesh. The plague of rats was gone—disappearing as suddenly as it had come.

Some said that the rats had simply eaten their

fill, and then gone back into the holes and burrows from which they had come. Others were convinced that the rats that had destroyed Bishop Hatto's grain, and Bishop Hatto himself, had been no ordinary rats. They believed that the rats were a Divine punishment for the horrible crime he had committed.

THE GHOST STEER

Cowboys around Brewster County, Texas, used to tell stories of a ghostly longhorn steer. The animal had an unusual brand on it; it read MURDER. Terrible things happened to anyone who had the misfortune to so much as glimpse the creature.

The story started in the year 1890. Two brothers, Zack and Gill Taylor, were rounding up longhorn cattle. The brothers had always been close, but they also had quick and fierce tempers. They often argued with one another.

The roundup had been a difficult one and the tempers of the brothers had been frayed by heat and fatigue. A dispute sprang up over the ownership of a magnificent longhorn steer.

"We could draw straws for him," said Gill.

"Or we could draw our guns," roared Zack. In a moment of unthinking rage, Zack whipped his six-shooter out of its holster and shot his younger brother dead.

Almost immediately Zack regretted what he had done and was overcome with grief and remorse. He wrapped his brother's body in a blanket and placed it over the back of a horse to carry it away for burial.

The cause of the dispute, the huge longhorn steer, remained unbranded. One of the cowhands un-thinkingly asked Zack what brand should be put on the animal.

"Put the same brand on him that I've got on my hide," said Zack. "Brand him MURDER and turn him loose. I hope he haunts this mesa for a thousand years."

Zack buried his brother that afternoon; then shot himself with the same gun he had used to kill Gill. And so the legend of the steer called Murder began.

Within a few months there were reports through-out the area of a ghostly longhorn, with a brand read-ing MURDER still fresh and raw on its side. According to the stories the sightings always sparked violence.

A cowboy saw the ghostly animal. When he told his two friends about it, they didn't believe him and called him a liar. He became so enraged at the insult that he shot them both.

A rancher was said to have killed his brother-in-law in a family argument just a few hours after he had sighted the steer.

A runaway boy who had determined to become a gunman saw the steer on a lonely trail. It frightened him so badly that he decided to turn himself in to the sheriff in the nearest town. When he tried to hand over his guns to the sheriff, the gesture was misinterpreted, and the sheriff shot the boy dead.

One of the last known stories about the ghost steer comes from around 1920. Lon Allen and his partner Cole Farrell owned a small ranch. It was next to a much larger spread owned by a man called Faye Dow. Dow wanted Allen and Farrell's land to add to his own, but he knew the partners would never sell. So he hatched a murderous plot. Pretending to be a friend, he convinced Allen that his partner was trying to steal his girl. He then told the hot-tempered Allen that the best thing to do would be to ambush Farrell.

One night Allen crouched behind some rocks near the trail that he knew Farrell would use when returning to the ranch. He heard hoofbeats and raised his gun, ready to shoot. But what was coming down the moonlit trail was not Clay Farrell on his horse, but a large longhorn steer bearing the brand of MURDER.

In a panic Allen fired four shots into the creature's skull. It didn't fall. It didn't even blink. It just looked at him sadly and trotted off into the darkness.

Dow heard the shots and assumed that Allen had killed his partner. He rushed to the scene of the shooting, but instead of finding a dead Clay Farrell, he found Lon Allen in a state of shock. Allen quickly recovered his senses, and then it didn't take him long to figure out what had happened: Faye Dow had tried to trick him into murdering his partner. When Allen fully realized how he had been tricked, he turned his gun on Dow and killed him.

In a very strange trial Allen defended not only himself, but the ghostly longhorn. He said that Farrell had indeed been riding down the trail, and if the phantom had not appeared first he would have been killed.

The jury took only ten minutes to acquit Allen.

After that there were few reports of sighting the phantom longhorn.

THE KING
OF THE
CATS

The legend of the King of the Cats is a very ancient and popular one. There have been many different versions of the story. This particular version appeared in a collection of Irish lore published about a century ago, but it is based on much older stories.

Some of the accounts in this book might be true. This one most certainly is not. But it's a good story anyway.

A couple of young men went on a hunting vacation in the Highlands of Scotland. They stayed at a small hunting lodge that was run by an old woman. The only other company in the house were the woman's large black cat and a hunting dog.

On one rather gloomy day one of the young men decided that he didn't feel up to tramping around in the outdoors. The other took the dog and went out to follow a trail that he had been on the previous day. He didn't want to make a long day of it. He said he would be back well before dark, and since it was late autumn in northern Scotland, dark came pretty early.

But the sun set, and the young man didn't come back. His companion had become rather worried. When the hunter finally returned, he was cold, wet and hungry, and was unwilling to talk much about why he was so late. He sat down to his supper which he ate in morose silence.

The food seemed to improve his mood a bit. When he finished he sat down with his companion in front of the fire. The dog was lying in the corner, and the cat was curled up comfortably on the hearth rug. Warm, relaxed and well fed, he began to talk.

"I know you must be wondering what happened to me," he said. "I hardly know how to tell you, it was so strange. I followed the track I meant to take and picked up a few birds, and it was well before sunset when I turned for home. Then one of those mountain mists came down, and I got right off the track and wandered around I don't know where until it was nearly dark. The dog seemed as puzzled as I was and kept following trails here and there, until I saw a light in the distance and made for it.

"Just as I got up to it, it seemed to disappear, but I was near a great old hollow oak, so I scrambled up the tree, thinking I might get a glimpse of the light from higher up. And as I climbed up I saw that the light was streaming up from the tree itself. So I scrambled up higher to look down into the hollow, and there I saw the strangest sight . . ."

At this point he stopped and looked over toward the fireplace. "Just look at that cat! He's listening to me! I swear he understands every word I'm saying!" And sure enough old Blackie had uncurled himself and was sitting straight up on the rug, staring intently at the young man, as only a cat can.

"Never mind the cat," said his friend, "tell me what happened."

"When I looked down into the tree it seemed as if I were looking down into a church," said the young man. "It was like a miniature church, with lights and an altar, and in front of the altar was a freshly dug hole, like an open grave.

"Then I heard sounds, a kind of howling and wailing. The dog began to get very excited and started howling himself, and scratching the tree. The sound came nearer and then I saw a procession enter the church—it was a procession of cats. Yes—cats."

At this point both men looked over at the hearth rug where the black cat was sitting alert and motionless. "It seemed to be a funeral procession, because the cats in front of the procession were carrying a small coffin. And what is even stranger is that a crown and scepter were on top of the coffin . . ."

Suddenly Blackie rose up on his hind legs and shouted: "Finally, Old Peter's dead, and I'm King of the Cats." With that he jumped through the window and was never seen again.

There are a number of other stories attached to the King of the Cats. A late-nineteenth-century book of Irish folklore and legends collected by Lady Speranza Wilde says that the King of the Cats may be any cat.

"He may be in your house, a common-looking fellow enough, with no distinguishing mark of exalted rank about him, so that it is very difficult to verify his genuine claim to royalty. Therefore the best way is to cut off a tiny little bit of his ear." (A reminder here, this is strictly a legend, so don't even think about cutting off a piece of your cat's ear!)

"If he is really the royal personage, he will immediately speak out and declare who he is; and perhaps, at the same time, tell you some very disagreeable truths about yourself, not at all pleasant to have discussed by the house cat."

Lady Wilde then goes on to relate the story of one man who in a drunken rage cut off the head of his pet cat and threw it in the fire. This turned out to be a big mistake, for this was no ordinary cat. From the fire a fierce voice growled, "Go tell your wife that you have cut off the head of the King of the Cats. But wait! I shall be avenged for this insult." The eyes of the cat glared at him hideously from the blaze.

You would think an experience like that would be

enough to put a man off cats forever. But not this fellow. He soon got another kitten. One evening he was playing with it when suddenly the once playful and docile kitten sank its fangs into his throat. The bite was well aimed, for it severed an artery and within moments the man bled to death.